A Short-Term **DISC**

D0193593

INVITATION
NEW TO THE TESTAMENT

LEADER GUIDE

Abingdon Press
Nashville

A SHORT-TERM DISCIPLE BIBLE STUDY

INVITATION TO THE NEW TESTAMENT
LEADER GUIDE

Copyright © 2005 by Abingdon Press

ISBN 13: 978-0-687-05498-5

Harriett Jane Olson, Editorial Director, Abingdon Press
Mark Price, Senior Editor
Cindy Caldwell, Development Editor
Kent Sneed, Design Manager

10 11 12 13 14 — 10 9 8 7 6 5 4 3

MANUFACTURED IN THE UNITED STATES OF AMERICA

Contents

Introduction

INVITATION TO THE NEW TESTAMENT is one of a series of studies developed on the model of DISCIPLE Bible study. DISCIPLE is a family of Bible study resources based on the general assumption that people are hungry for God's Word, for fellowship in prayer and study, and for biblically informed guidance in ministry. This series of Short-Term DISCIPLE Bible Studies, like the long-term DISCIPLE series, (1) presents the Bible as the primary text, (2) calls for daily preparation on the part of students, (3) features a weekly meeting based on small group discussion, (4) includes a video component for making available the insights of biblical scholars to set the Scriptures in context, and (5) has as one of its goals the enhancement of Christian discipleship.

INVITATION TO THE NEW TESTAMENT is designed to provide congregations with an in-depth, high-commitment Bible study resource able to be completed in a shorter time frame than the foundational DISCIPLE studies. The shorter time frame, however, does not mean this study has expectations different from those associated with the thirty-four week DISCIPLE: BECOMING DISCIPLES THROUGH BIBLE STUDY. The expectation remains that participants will prepare for the weekly meeting by reading substantial portions of Scripture and taking notes. The expectation remains that group discussion, rather than lecture, will be the preferred learning approach. The expectation remains that biblical scholarship will be part of the group's study together. The expectation remains that persons' encounter with the Bible will call them to more faithful discipleship. Hopefully, in fact, one of the chief benefits of the Short-Term DISCIPLE Bible Studies, will be how well they inspire persons to commit to a long-term DISCIPLE study in the future. While short-term studies of selected Scriptures can be both meaningful and convenient, the deeply transforming experience of reading and studying substantial portions of Scriptures, for a sustained period of time, continues to be the primary aim of DISCIPLE.

Leading This Study

As leaders of INVITATION TO THE NEW TESTAMENT, keep in mind that to have as rich and meaningful a study experience as possible with this type of short-term study, you will need to pay close attention to the timing of the suggested discussion activities and group dynamics. One of the challenges of any short-term, small-group study—especially one based on group discussion—is the time it takes for people in the study to become comfortable sharing with one another. If your group is made up of people who are already acquainted, the challenge may be minimal. However, be prepared to have a group of people who do not know one another well, perhaps some who have never done much substantive Bible study, and others who are graduates of long-term DISCIPLE studies. Make use of the following information as you prepare to lead INVITATION TO THE NEW TESTAMENT:

GROUP ORIENTATION

Plan to schedule an orientation meeting a week prior to the first weekly meeting. Take time then to make introductions, discuss the expectations of the study, distribute and preview the materials, and review the upcoming week's assignment. If necessary, consider discussing the kind of study Bible group members should use and taking time to be sure everyone is familiar with the aids in a study Bible. Have on hand several types of study Bibles for persons to look through. Also, as part of your group's orientation, consider viewing the brief introduction to the study that appears just before Video Segment 1, Part 1.

THE WEEKLY SESSION

The times in parentheses, beneath each section heading in the leader guide planning pages, indicate the suggested number of minutes to allow for a particular activity. The first time is for use with a 60-minute meeting schedule, and the second time is for use with a 90-minute meeting. Keep in mind that it is always possible the discussion questions suggested for use in any one section will be more than enough to take up the allotted time. The leader will need to keep an eye on a clock and decide when and whether to move on. The best way to gauge, in advance, how many questions to use and how long to allow discussion to last is to spend time answering the suggested questions while preparing for the group session. Be sure to do that as well as preview the video, both Part 1 and Part 2, before the weekly session.

Gathering Around God's Word
(15 – 20 minutes)

Welcome
Begin on time by welcoming the group to the study. Ideally, this should be the *second* time the group has been together. During the orientation meeting the previous week, group participants met to preview the materials, discuss expectations of the study, and receive the assignment for the week. In case group participants arrive at this first session who were not present at the orientation meeting, be prepared to summarize as briefly as possible what they can expect from the study and what the study will expect from them.

Invitation to the Table (Optional)
In keeping with the theme of invitation, each week consider setting up a small table somewhere in the meeting room. The table will serve as a focal point for the group. The suggestions in this section include a list of what to place on the table and an opening question for reflection and brief discussion. Both the question and the table items are designed to connect a central theme of the week's study with the participants' own experience. While this is an option for the group, it may well serve to establish a sense of community within the group.

Prayer
Establish a particular ritual of praying together at the start of the study. Keep in mind that the text of this study, the Bible, is a rich source of mean-

ingful prayers. Many of the New Testament letters the group will study contain a hymn or a prayer. Make use of appropriate texts from the Psalms or some of the words spoken by Jesus in the Gospels. When appropriate, make use of other Bible translations when praying the Scriptures. A suggestion of both a New Testament text and a psalm text will appear in this section each week; but feel free to choose another. Be sure to include group members in this process by inviting those participants who are willing to lead in prayer.

Viewing the Video: Session 1, Part 1

The video component in the series has two parts and both parts are central to the group's study. Part 1 is a ten-minute presentation by one of the writers of the participant book commentary on some topic related to the Scriptures and themes in the week's readings. The purpose of this video is to provide a common base of information about or interpretation of the Scriptures for the group to discuss. A brief summary of this video appears in the leader guide plan for each session.

Encountering God's Word in the Text

(20 – 25 minutes)

In this section, group discussion centers on some of the Scripture passages read during the week.

Examining God's Word in Context

(15 – 20 minutes)

Viewing the Video: Session 1, Part 2

The focus in this section is on viewing Part 2 of the video. This video features an informal, unscripted, roundtable conversation between the two writers of the study and a guest scholar. Like Part 1, this conversation pertains to some theme that emerges from the week's readings and is designed to stimulate further discussion. The first question for group discussion appears on screen at the conclusion of the segment. That same question appears first, in *italics*, in the leader guide plan for each session, along with additional questions for further discussion. **Note:** An intentional characteristic of Part 2 is its informality. As a result, on occasion the presenters may stumble over a word or jumble a phrase. Be aware of that. Sometimes retaining the flow of a conversation was more advisable than trying to excise a verbal miscue.

Going Forth with God's Word:
An Invitation to Discipleship
(10 – 15 minutes)

Consideration of the implications of the week's readings on the call of Christian discipleship is the point of this section. The discussion questions in the leader guide plan for each session come from questions raised in the commentary and the "For Reflection" sections of the participant book. Be alert to additional questions that come to mind and might be useful at this time in the group meeting.

Closing and Prayer

Turn to the next session and review the focus of the lesson and the assignments for the week ahead. Establish a pattern of inviting prayer concerns and praying together at this time.

GROUP DYNAMICS

The effectiveness of the group's study together depends heavily upon the way you, as the leader, manage individual participation. Plan for the majority of the weekly discussion to take place in smaller groups of three or four or in pairs. Smaller groupings will give everyone more opportunity to talk and is the best way for people to get to know one another quickly. Smaller groupings will reduce the possibility that a couple of people will dominate the conversation or that some will not contribute at all. Smaller groupings communicate that preparation is expected and essential for fruitful discussion.

Also key to the effectiveness of the group's study together is how you manage your role as the leader. Remember: your primary role is to facilitate the process, not to provide the information. To that end, follow these basic guidelines as you lead the study:

- Prepare exactly as participant's prepare; see yourself as a learner among learners.
- Know where the discussion is heading from the outset; this will minimize the chances of getting sidetracked along the way.
- Set ground rules for group participation and maintenance early on; doing so will encourage the whole group to take responsibility for monitoring itself.
- Be a good listener; don't be afraid of silence—allow time for people to think before responding.

JESUS CALLS US INTO GOD'S REDEMPTION STORY

SESSION

1

Gathering Around God's Word
(15 – 20 minutes)

Welcome
Begin on time by welcoming the group to the study. Ideally this should be the *second* time the group has been together. During the orientation meeting the previous week, group participants met to preview the materials, discuss expectations of the study, and receive the assignment for the week. In case group participants who were not present at the orientation meeting arrive at this first session be prepared to summarize as briefly as possible what they can expect from the study and what the study will expect from them.

Invitation to the Table (Optional)
In keeping with the theme of invitation, each week set up a small table somewhere in the meeting room. The table will serve as a thematic focal point for the group. The suggestions in this section include a list of what to place on the table and an opening question for reflection and brief discussion. Both the question and the table items are designed to connect a central theme of the week's study with the participants' own experience.

- **Opening question:** What establishes your identity?
- **Items for the table:** birth certificate, driver's license, passport, scrapbook, family picture, family Bible

Prayer
Establish a particular ritual of praying together at the start of the study. Keep in mind that the text of this study, the Bible, is a rich source of mean-

ingful prayers. Many of the New Testament letters the group will study contain a hymn or a prayer. Make use of appropriate texts from the Psalms or some of the words spoken by Jesus in the Gospels. When appropriate, make use for other Bible translations when praying the Scriptures. A suggestion for both a New Testament text and a psalm text will appear in this section each week; but feel free to choose another. Be sure to include group members in this process by inviting those participants who are willing to lead in prayer.

- *Hebrews 1:1-3 or Psalm 91:14-16*

Viewing the Video: Session 1, Part 1

Prepare to View Video
Listen for the part the New Testament plays in the Bible's story about God.

Summary of Video Content:
The themes from Matthew's story of Jesus determine the conversation topics for our study. The daily reading assignments move between Gospel passages and related New Testament passages. The video segments present an interpretation of some theme or topic raised by the readings via presentation by a single scholar and also a roundtable discussion by several scholars.

At the heart of this study is Jesus. The coming of Jesus – his life, actions, mission, death, and resurrection—was the fundamental element for all writers of the New Testament.

The Christian Bible contains both an "old" and "new" testament, both of which are part of the same continuous story. It is a story about God from beginning to end. In the New Testament, God's mission becomes embodied in the person of Jesus the Galilean. The New Testament writers wrestled with the Hebrew Scriptures in order to interpret the importance of God's mission in the world and the role of the people of God in it.

Discuss After Viewing Video:
What part does the New Testament play in telling the Bible's story of God's mission in the world? How does thinking of Jesus' coming as the lens through which the New Testament writers read the story of God affect how we read that story?

Encountering God's Word in the Text
(20 – 25 minutes)

The emphasis in this lesson is on the claims made about Jesus' identity and, because of these claims, how Jesus calls us into God's redemption story. Form four small groups and make the following assignments: Group 1: Matthew 1–4 (Day 1 readings); Group 2: Luke 1–4 (Day 2 readings); Group 3: Acts 2:22-39; 3:13-26; Galatians 3 (Day 3 readings); Group 4: John 1; Hebrews 1–2 (Day 4 readings). Instruct the groups to discuss their Scripture assignment, using their daily notes, in relation to these questions: What claims are being made about Jesus' identity? What impact do these claims about Jesus have on our relationship with God? How do the responses of the people who encounter the Jesus in these passages support these claims?

When encountering Jesus, how we identify him often determines how we will respond to him. In new groups of three or four read John 6:22-71 and discuss these questions: What factors contribute to how a person responds to an encounter with Jesus? Since Jesus calls each of us into God's redemption story, "what must we do to perform the works of God?"

Examining God's Word in Context
(15 – 20 minutes)

The Gospel of Matthew opens the New Testament by pointing out that Jesus is deeply rooted in the story of Israel. In order for us to fully understand the call of Jesus into God's redemption story, we must pay attention to how the New Testament writers use the Old Testament as a frame of reference for understanding who Jesus is and how he fits into the whole biblical story.

Viewing the Video: Session 1, Part 2

Prepare to View Video:
Listen for what is said about the various ways Matthew and the New Testament writers read the Old Testament.

Discuss After Viewing Video:
How is reading the Old Testament on its own terms important for understanding the New Testament? "The New Testament writers are reading the

Old Testament and they're seeing that what God wants for people, what God expects of the obedient one, has taken on flesh in Jesus." What does this statement mean? What does this statement say about the connection between the Old Testament and the New Testament? How does this statement challenge the practice of reading the Old Testament "simply as a witness to what happens in Jesus"?

Going Forth with God's Word:
An Invitation to Discipleship
(10 – 15 minutes)

Like the earliest believers, when we encounter Jesus, we are confronted with various claims concerning his identity and significance. Our response may vary, but how we respond is important. In pairs, discuss the following questions: How do you respond to Jesus' question, "Who do you say that I am?" How does what you believe about Jesus inform how you follow him in discipleship?

Conclude the group's discussion by calling attention to the "For Reflection" section on page 22 in the participant book. Ask the group to form pairs and share responses to one or more of the questions at the end of that section.

Closing and Prayer

Turn to Session 2, Review the focus of the lesson and the assignments for the week ahead. Establish a pattern of inviting prayer concerns and praying together at this time.

JESUS CALLS US TO A TRANSFORMED LIFE

Gathering Around God's Word
(15 – 20 minutes)

Welcome
Begin on time by welcoming the group to the study.

Invitation to the Table (Optional)
- **Opening question:** What images come to mind when you think of transformation?
- **Items for the table:** flower bulb, picture of butterfly, picture of seashore, picture of baby

Prayer
- *Matthew 5:14-16 or Psalm 1:1-3*

Viewing the Video: Session 2, Part 1

Prepare to View Video
Listen for what it means to be a part of God's kingdom through the direction of Jesus.

Summary of Video Content:
The Sermon on the Mount is the most familiar of Jesus' speeches. It appears only in the Gospel of Matthew.

The sermon lays out examples of what it means to be part of God's kingdom through the direction of Jesus and establishes guidelines on how to develop and maintain relationships in the new realm of God. The teachings involve other persons, those inside and outside the community of faith. To "do unto others as you would have them do to you" applies to everyone.

Jesus came not to abolish the law but to fulfill it. In his teachings, he sharpens or tightens the law.

The point of the whole sermon might well be summed up in a single sentence: "Be perfect therefore, as your heavenly Father is perfect." To be "perfect" means to treat people fairly and with consistency and kindness despite how they may have acted toward us.

Discuss After Viewing Video:

How does the Sermon on the Mount describe a life in community with God and with others? "For Matthew, Jesus is the new Moses." What does this statement suggest about how Jesus' followers are to view and respond to his teachings?

Encountering God's Word in the Text

(20 – 25 minutes)

The readings this week describe the contrast between behaviors that are in keeping with life in God and behaviors that are more in keeping with an untransformed life. Form three groups. Ask one group to scan Matthew 5–7 to identify behaviors of an untransformed life and behaviors of a transformed life. Ask the second group to scan James 1–5 with the same instructions. Ask the third group to scan Romans 1–8 with the same instructions. Procedure suggestion: for ease of reporting, have the groups list the two sets of behaviors in two columns on a sheet of paper.

After the groups have compiled their lists, allow them an opportunity to share their findings with the total group.

Ask everyone to turn to Matthew 5:21-48. Form two groups and have them stand facing each other. Instruct persons from one group to locate the portions of the passage that begin with the words, "*you have heard that it was said....*" Then instruct persons from the facing group to locate the portions that follow with the words, "*but I say to you....*" Have the groups then begin reading the passages aloud in this manner: one person from one group reads a "*you have heard that it was said...*" passage, followed by a person from the other group reading a "but I say to you..." passage. Follow this sequence to read through the end of the text.

According to the Scripture readings this week, the transformed life is more than just following the Law. Yet Jesus claims to have come not to abolish the Law but to fulfill it. In two groups, discuss this question: How does the Law function for followers of Jesus?

Examining God's Word in Context
(15 – 20 minutes)

Jesus teaches that the righteousness God calls for extends to speech, to attitude, and even to how we perceive other people. In order to embody this righteousness, an individual must be lifted up and empowered. We are lifted up through Christ who became the sacrifice that reconciles sinners and God. We are empowered by the Spirit, which enables us to do what the Law requires. The Spirit also provides guidance and power to live righteous lives before God and with one another.

Viewing the Video: Session 2, Part 2

Prepare to View Video:
Listen for the role that faith and works play in righteous living.

Discuss After Viewing Video:
What do Jesus, Paul, and James say about the relationship between faith and works? What characterizes a life of faith? What impact do works have (or should have) on one's faith?

Going Forth with God's Word:
An Invitation to Discipleship
(10-15 minutes)

Doing what God wants instead of what we want often calls for changes in our attitude and/or behavior. Jesus calls us to a transformed life. So do James and Paul. In pairs, discuss the following questions: Which of the week's scriptural perspectives—Jesus' (Matthew), James's, or Paul's—most challenges your way of life? What aspect of living a transformed life do you find most difficult? How would you explain to others on their journey of faith that doing what God wants brings freedom, not limits, into life?

Ask the group to pair up and discuss this question: What areas in your life do you tend to resist the thought of God asking you to change?

Closing and Prayer

Turn to Session 3. Review the focus of the lesson and the assignments for the week ahead. Close with prayer.

JESUS CALLS US TO MINISTER TO A HOSTILE WORLD

Gathering Around God's Word
(15 – 20 minutes)

Welcome
Begin on time by welcoming the group to the study.

Invitation to the Table (Optional)
• **Opening question:** How has your world changed in the past five years?
• **Items for the table:** world globe or map, newspapers showing headlines of shootings, picture of gun, picture of graffiti, picture of prisoner

Prayer
• **Acts 4:24b-29 or Psalm 19:8-15**

Viewing the Video: Session 3, Part 1

Prepare to View Video
Listen for the various ways the word that is translated "gospel" has been used throughout history and in Scripture.

Summary of Video Content:
The Greek word *euangelion* that is translated as "gospel" did not at first refer to a written "life of Jesus." It was used extensively in the Classical world whenever a messenger brought welcome and anxiously anticipated news. The plural of *euangelion* (*euangelia*) could be used to refer to the rewards for delivering good news that pertained to a whole city. The verb

form of the word *euangelion*, "gospel," describes the announcement in Isaiah 52:7 that God was about to lead the Jewish exiles out of captivity and back to their homeland.

In the Roman period, *euangelion* was occasionally associated with the reign of the emperor. Augustus's birthday was said to "signal the beginning of the good news for the world." For Jesus, the "good news" was that God's kingdom was now dawning, breaking in to supplant all the domination systems of the world by calling people to a radically new vision for life together. Christian missionaries bear "good news" in that the promises made by the Hebrew prophets had come to fruition at last in the life and work of Jesus.

Unlike some messengers, Paul announces this good news with a view to pleasing the one whose reign he announces, rather than pleasing the hearers in the hope of being accepted and even rewarded by them. Jesus himself had warned that messengers might lose their lives for the sake of witnessing to this "good news," precisely the reward for bearing bad news. The Christian "good news" nurtured a profound interest in the life and teaching of the leader whom they followed from life to death to life again.

Discuss After Viewing Video:

What is the gospel or "good news" that Jesus came to share? How does this "good news" compare with the gospel the church is sharing today? In what ways do you think our world hears the "good news" of Jesus as bad news?

Encountering God's Word in the Text
(20 – 25 minutes)

The emphasis in this lesson is on the ministry of Jesus, the forming of a community of followers of Jesus, and the ministry of the Christian community in the world. Hear Matthew 10:32-42 read aloud. Then choose one of these two options to study the passage in groups of three. Option One: Instruct participants to rewrite the passage in their own words. Then ask for volunteers to read their paraphrase to the entire group. Option Two: Have groups of three discuss the message of Matthew 10:32-42 using notes from their reading and study with this question as a guide: What words of Jesus in this passage shake up your ideas of discipleship?

As a total group, recall the readings from Acts 1–5. Talk about the difficulties faced by the early believers as they tried to form community and share the good news. To what extent do their difficulties mirror those facing believers today?

Hear 1 Thessalonians 1–2:8 read aloud, listening to it as a love letter to a congregation. Then ask persons to share the kind of response Paul's words evoke from them.

Examining God's Word in Context
(15 – 20 minutes)

In the new community where God reigns, humility and service—not force—lead to greatness. The community is a witness to the presence of God's reign in the world, a reign that involves reconceptions of, and challenges to all earthly power structures.

Viewing the Video: Session 3, Part 2

Prepare to View Video:
Listen for ways the culture threatens the Christian community and ways the Christian community threatens the culture.

Discuss After Viewing Video:
To what extent does the church today face opposition? Does the Christian community not see opposition from Western culture because that culture reflects the values of Jesus? How so? Or have we lost our way and our distinctive witness and we no longer pose a threat to those around us? How so? What direction is the Christian community heading in our day?

Going Forth with God's Word:
An Invitation to Discipleship
(10 – 15 minutes)

In Matthew, Jesus says, "I desire mercy not sacrifice." He says this not once but twice. This does not imply that sacrifice has been abolished as unnecessary but that mercy is a more important activity wherever these two are in tension. For Jesus, *mercy* means that it is preferable to do good and act kindly toward one's fellow human beings than not to act because of the hindrance of some religious observance.

In pairs, discuss the following questions: What is the ministry you are called to perform in a hostile world? Would you describe this ministry as an act of mercy or an act of sacrifice? What support do you have as you carry out this ministry?

Conclude the group's discussion by calling attention to the "For Reflection" section on page 42 in the participant book. Ask the group to stay in pairs and share responses to the last question in that section.

Closing and Prayer

Turn to Session 4. Review the focus of the lesson and the assignments for the week ahead. Close with prayer.

JESUS CALLS US TO COMPLEX COMMUNITIES OF FAITH

Gathering Around God's Word
(15 – 20 minutes)

Welcome
Begin on time by welcoming the group to the study.

Invitation to the Table (Optional)
- **Opening question:** How do you define *diversity*?
- **Items for the table:** pictures of people of various races, star of David, copy of the Quran, the Bible, a picture of the church

Prayer
- *1 John 1:1-3 or Psalm 98:4-9*

Viewing the Video: Session 4, Part 1

Prepare to View Video
Listen for the two ways in which Christians in the early church understood their participation in the community of faith and being holy in the world.

Summary of Video Content:
In the church of Antioch, some Jewish Christians rebuked those who ate at the same table with Gentile Christians. This was ignoring the boundaries between Jews and Gentiles. Eating only certain foods prepared in certain ways, abstaining from all work on the seventh day, and circumcising their male children were practices that set Jews apart from other people groups.

The decisive proof that the Judaizers were on the wrong track was the fact that God was giving the Holy Spirit to Gentile Christians while they were still uncircumcised. Falling in line with what God is doing, then, would require precisely the opposite of what it did in Leviticus. It would involve treating as clean those whom God had treated as clean and witnessing to God's acceptance of the Gentiles even in the face of persecution.

The incident at Antioch and the trouble in Galatia reflect the debate between two positions concerning how God's people were to mirror God's holiness, and how Gentiles found a place in that people. Paul's position had the vision to transform a faith bound up with a particular ethnic group into a faith that could bind together people from every ethnic group, language, and nation.

Discuss After Viewing Video:

What was the issue in the church in Antioch and in the church in Galatia? What was at stake in resolving the issue? What position on the issue did Paul take in each case? What similar issues arise in the life of the church today, and how do we respond to them?

Encountering God's Word in the Text
(20 – 25 minutes)

As a community of faith, our focus should be on the mission in the world, "doing the will of God," and not on the specific compatibility of each member with the rest of the body. Many of us would rather exclude others unlike us. In groups of four, using Galatians 5–6 as a focal text (and using notes made on the other readings), write a statement of covenant for a Christian community of faith that reflects the message of the Galatians text. Have each group select someone to share its covenant statement with the whole group.

Hear Matthew 15:1-9 and 15:21-28 read aloud. Then discuss this question: What does Jesus' criticism of the "tradition of the elders" and his acceptance of the faith of a Gentile woman say about Jesus' mission?

Examining God's Word in Context
(15 – 20 minutes)

It's very easy to be Christian in a neighborhood where everybody else is Christian; but when we move out to the wider world, it is much more difficult to maintain our own identity.

Viewing the Video: Session 4, Part 2

Prepare to View Video:
Listen for what is said about multiculturalism and ethnic diversity in churches in the twenty-first century.

Discuss After Viewing Video:
How do we maintain both unity and diversity in the body of Christ? How can the church in the twenty-first century be a kind of community where we welcome people, recognize each other's cultural concerns, and celebrate the diversity of God's people?

Going Forth with God's Word:
An Invitation to Discipleship
(10 – 15 minutes)

God does not call a community of faith to maintain the status quo. God's call and reign is far bigger that any program or outreach event we plan. God may even force us out of comfortable places in order for us to turn to God for wisdom and strategy. In groups of three or four, talk about the church's struggle with the question of how much cultural accommodation to allow. Then discuss how the church defines God's mission in the world today and what "comfort zones" we find most difficult to leave in order for all to be welcomed at God's table.

Conclude the group's discussion by calling attention to the "For Reflection" section on page 52 in the participant book. Ask the group to form pairs and share responses to the last two questions in that section.

Closing and Prayer

Turn to Session 5. Review the focus of the lesson and the assignments for the week ahead. Close with prayer.

JESUS CALLS US TO SERVE ONE ANOTHER

Gathering Around God's Word
(15 – 20 minutes)

Welcome
Begin on time by welcoming the group to the study.

Invitation to the Table (Optional)
• **Opening question:** What is your understanding of service?
• **Items for the table:** towel and basin of water, paint brush, hammer, greeting card

Prayer
• *2 Thessalonians 3:16-17 or Psalm 146:5-10*

Viewing the Video: Session 5, Part 1

Prepare to View Video
Listen for what is said about the various messianic expectations during the intertestamental period and how Jesus fulfilled these expectations.

Summary of Video Content:
The period between the testaments was a fertile time for messianic hopes, as people reached for some vision of how God would bring about the promises proclaimed in their Scriptures. Jesus laid claim to being the Messiah. But Jesus' teaching concerning his own messiahship shows a Messiah who understood that God's vision for human community could not be brought about or sustained by the same means as every other domi-

nation system on the face of the globe. Rather, Jesus came as a self-giving Messiah, whose ransoming death would make enemies into part of the chosen people and whose serving would provide a new model for the use of power. In this new model, the path to fullness is through self-emptying, and the path to personal worth and value is through recognizing and nurturing the worth and value of all those around us.

Discuss After Viewing Video:

How would our understanding of discipleship be changed if Jesus had come as a military Messiah? as a priestly Messiah? How does knowing Jesus as a self-giving Messiah affect our understanding and practice of discipleship?

Encountering God's Word in the Text
(20 – 25 minutes)

In a world filled with reminders of how the body of Christ ought not to live, this lesson reminds us that we serve a self-giving Messiah who calls us to serve one another. Form two groups and make the following assignments: Group 1: Scan the assigned readings in Matthew 17–20 and identify the conflicts that arise among the disciples and how they are addressed by Jesus. Group 2: Scan the assigned readings in First and Second Corinthians and Second Thessalonians and identify the conflicts in those churches and how they are addressed by Paul. Come together as a total group to discuss this question: What do Jesus and Paul teach us about how to address conflicts in our own churches?

Consider Paul's discussion of stewardship and generosity in 2 Corinthians 8–9. First, hear 2 Corinthians 8:7-15 and 2 Corinthians 9:6-12 read aloud. Then have pairs share their understanding of what these two passages say about Christ and what it means to be the church.

Examining God's Word in Context
(15 – 20 minutes)

There is no discipleship with Jesus without discipline and without being willing to risk community with one another. This is a community where people actively seek out, confront, and engage in issues, and then respond.

Viewing the Video: Session 5, Part 2

Prepare to View Video:
Listen for what is said about the church as community.

Discuss After Viewing Video:
How is dealing with conflict in the church a part of discipleship? What has been your experience of conflict within the Christian community? What actions or attitudes are called for on the part of Christians to be willing to risk community with one another?

Going Forth with God's Word:
An Invitation to Discipleship
(10 – 15 minutes)

In an individualistic society, Jesus calls us not to be served but to serve. In pairs, discuss the following questions: What do you think serving one another means today? How can the church's call to serving or ministering to one another sometimes differ from the call of Jesus?

Conclude the group's discussion by calling attention to the "For Reflection" section on page 62 in the participant book. Ask the group to form pairs and share responses to the last question in that section.

Closing and Prayer

Turn to Session 6. Review the focus of the lesson and the assignments for the week ahead. Close with prayer.

JESUS CALLS US TO A NEW RELATIONSHIP WITH TRADITION

Gathering Around God's Word
(15 – 20 minutes)

Welcome
Begin on time by welcoming the group to the study.

Invitation to the Table (Optional)
- **Opening question:** What are some of your family traditions?
- **Items for the table:** picture of family gathered around table, a Christmas card, a box wrapped with Christmas wrapping, a lighted candle)

Prayer
- **Romans 11:33-36 or Psalm 79:9-13**

Viewing the Video: Session 6, Part 1

Prepare to View Video
Listen for what is said about the relationship between the people of the new covenant (church) and the people of the old covenant (Israel).

Summary of Video Content:
The Qumran community was in conflict with its host society about the meaning of their shared tradition. They had entered into the "new covenant." Yet, the "new covenant" is itself an ancient, traditional concept. It derives its meaningfulness from the former covenant in two ways. First, the notion that God relates to God's people through a covenant con-

nects the new with the old. And second, the new covenant is seen to be nothing other than the renewal and the internalization of the former covenant.

The lines of the new covenant are now drawn around the outpouring of God's favor in Jesus and in the giving of the Holy Spirit. Terms from the first covenant operate as a framework that gives meaning to the new covenant: the circumcision, Abraham's offspring, a chosen race, a royal priesthood, a holy nation, God's peculiar possession, Israel.

The statements made by early Christians do not reflect a rejection of tradition, but rather a debate about how to be faithful to the tradition and thus how to continue to respond faithfully to God. The scriptural tradition reflected in both testaments provides an enduring compass point for navigating a path of faithful response to the God who engages us anew in the present.

Discuss After Viewing Video:

How does tradition function as a "compass point for navigating a path of faithful response to God"? What are some examples of how we appropriate past traditions in order to be faithful in the present? What can the Qumran community teach the Christian community about how to relate to tradition?

Encountering God's Word in the Text

(20 – 25 minutes)

Tradition often provides the lens through which we read the Bible. In groups of three or four discuss the kinds of religious traditions (e.g., church teachings or doctrines, congregational polity and practices) that exist in the body of Christ and how these traditions inform our interpretation of the Bible. What impact (either positive or negative) do some of these traditions have on the body of Christ?

Form two groups. Have one group focus on Matthew 22–23, looking for what Jesus defines as the benefits and the limits of tradition; have the other group focus on Romans 9–11, looking for what Paul defines as the benefits and the limits of tradition. Ask both groups to make a list of their findings.

Once both groups finish their work, come together as a total group. Hear both groups report their findings and then talk about how Jesus' and Paul's views of tradition compare. Finally, consider this question: In the church today, what determines which traditions to abandon or to keep?

Examining God's Word in Context
(15 – 20 minutes)

Jews define the Messiah differently than Christians do. What is self-evident to one group is incomprehensible to the other.

Viewing the Video: Session 6, Part 2

Prepare to View Video:
Listen for the elements that are common and the elements that separate Jews and Christians.

Discuss After Viewing Video:
As Christians, how should we relate to Jews? How does the idea that Jesus' conflict with Jewish leaders was an "in-house" dispute address the issue of how Christians relate to Jews? How is the Christian sign of the "new" covenant (baptism) like and unlike the Jewish sign of the "old" covenant (circumcision)? How might those similarities or differences inform the way Christians relate to Jews?

Going Forth with God's Word: An Invitation to Discipleship
(10 – 15 minutes)

Tradition itself represents a story about the way those in the past have discovered their own faithful expression of the work of God among them. The struggle with tradition is essential to faithful living in Christ. In pairs, discuss the following questions: What religious traditions (teachings, practices, beliefs) have actually hindered your faith? What religious traditions have strengthened your faith?

Conclude the group's discussion by calling attention to the "For Reflection" section on page 72 in the participant book. Ask the group to form pairs and share responses to the first question in that section.

Closing and Prayer

Turn to Session 7. Review the focus of the lesson and the assignments for the week ahead. Close with prayer.

JESUS CALLS US TO LIVE IN LIGHT OF HIS COMING AGAIN

Gathering Around God's Word
(15 – 20 minutes)

Welcome
Begin on time by welcoming the group to the study.

Invitation to the Table (Optional)
- **Opening question:** What hymns come to mind when you think of Jesus coming back and heaven?
- **Items for the table:** Bible turned to Revelation, hymnbook turned to "There's a Land That is Fairer Than Day," picture of clouds, picture of cemetery

Prayer
- *Revelation 19:6b-8 or Psalm 86:8-13*

Viewing the Video: Session 7, Part 1

Prepare to View Video
Listen for the characteristics of apocalyptic writings.

Summary of Video Content:
Revelation is the only full-book example of a genre of writing known as an apocalypse. Portions of other books in this genre are: Matthew 24 and 2 Thessalonians 2. Traces of apocalyptic thought can be found in Ezekiel, Isaiah 24, and Daniel. The author of Daniel describes his period of history as the end of days and expects God and heavenly agents to intervene and

bring about Israel's triumph. Revelation shares a common theme that Christ's coming, called the *parousia,* will have ramifications for the end of the age.

Within all Christian appropriations of this type of language also comes a deep-seated sense of hope. These words of hope intermingle with the images of destruction, disaster, and loss as a forewarning to the people of God to stay on track and be encouraged. In the end, for all of the attempts by apocalyptic writings to imagine a more just world, they confirm that God stands at the center. This word of hope to a discouraged people is God's final word.

Discuss After Viewing Video:

What is your understanding of the apocalyptic writings in the Bible? What feelings are evoked when reading them? In what ways do the Bible's apocalyptic writings shape or inform your beliefs as a Christian?

Encountering God's Word in the Text
(20 – 25 minutes)

The most consistent feature of the various descriptions of the "end time" events found across the New Testament is the writers' conviction that disciples' priorities, investments, and ambitions should all be shaped by the knowledge of the "end." Being "ready" recurs throughout this literature as a constant refrain.

Form two groups. Instruct one group to review the four parables in Matthew 24:45–25:46 (the faithful slave; the ten bridesmaids; the talents; and the Great Judgment) and respond to the question, What does it mean to be "ready"? Instruct the other group to review Revelation 21 and respond to the question, "Ready" for what?

Allow time for each group to share its findings.

As a total group, review the readings assigned for Day 2 from First Thessalonians, Hebrews, and Second Peter. Talk about how the group responded to the question accompanying that day's assignment: How do you think the promise of Christ's return sustained the early Christians during their suffering? How does it sustain Christians today?

Conclude by hearing Revelation 22:12-17 read aloud while others follow along in their Bibles.

Examining God's Word in Context
(15 – 20 minutes)

In Revelation, the word that John is putting forth is certainly a word for his own immediate community. But it is also a word for the wider Christian community. It is a word for believers today.

Viewing the Video: Session 7, Part 2

Prepare to View Video:
Listen for ways in which Revelation and the New Testament confront systems of domination then and now.

Discuss After Viewing Video:
How is Revelation's critique of Roman oppression relevant to today's world? How do we use the Bible at times to justify, rather than judge, how we live? If we were to use the biblical text to "read" (that is, critique) our culture, what warnings or words of hope would we find?

Going Forth with God's Word:
An Invitation to Discipleship
(10 – 15 minutes)

Jesus' invitation is to live now in the assurance that he will come again. In living, we must continue to proclaim that we are all accountable to God for what we do and what we fail to do. In pairs, discuss how we become "ensnared by the priorities of living only for the present rather than focusing on the future." Jesus calls us to live in light of his coming again in the future. Talk about what this means for our life in the present.

Conclude the group's discussion by calling attention to the "For Reflection" section on page 82 in the participant book. Ask the group to form pairs and share responses to the last question in that section.

Closing and Prayer

Turn to Session 8. Review the focus of the lesson and the assignments for the week ahead. Close with prayer.

JESUS CALLS US TO EXPERIENCE THE GIFTS OF HIS DYING AND RISING

Gathering Around God's Word
(15 – 20 minutes)

Welcome
Begin on time by welcoming the group to the study.

Invitation to the Table (Optional)
- **Opening question:** How would you define life after death?
- **Items for the table:** cross, picture of empty tomb, Bible turned to Matthew 28, a potted plant filled with blooms, pictures of people doing stuff—eating, playing, and so forth

Prayer
- **Romans 8:37-39 or Psalm 22:25-31**

Viewing the Video: Session 8, Part 1

Prepare to View Video
Listen for perceptions of life after death and the Resurrection.

Summary of Video Content:
There is little within the Old Testament tradition that points in the direction of a clear belief in life after death. Most passages speak of a place called *Sheol*, where one is separated from the living and has no memory of God.

Hellenization had an impact on the view of life after death. Documents show stories speaking of a bodily resurrection after death and the immortality of the soul.

The proclamation that Jesus has risen from the dead was a proclamation of vindication that the Crucifixion was not the last word. All the Gospels depict empty tombs, if not appearances of Jesus, as a way of emphasizing bodily resurrection from the dead. Paul moves beyond vindication to affirm that Christ's resurrection also implies a general resurrection for all. For it is precisely in the resurrection of the Lord Jesus Christ, Paul says, that God defeats the final enemy, death.

Discuss After Viewing Video:
What is the Old Testament's view of life after death? What is the New Testament's view of life after death? What Scriptures most inform your view of life after death?

Encountering God's Word in the Text
(20 – 25 minutes)

Jesus performs the final and complete "Day of Atonement" ritual, sanctifying the people and going not into the earthly Temple but into the heavenly Holy of Holies. He goes there to remove the defilements caused by the sin of the people, offering his "body" as the perfection of the animal sacrifices that God rejected. By so doing, Jesus opened wide the way into "heaven itself," preparing us to live forever in the very presence of God.

In groups of three or four, compare and contrast Exodus 24:3-8 and Hebrews 8–10. Discuss how the writer of Hebrews uses Leviticus to interpret Jesus' death. What does the writer accomplish by explaining the significance of Jesus' death in the context of Israel's sacrificial system? Talk about the meaning of the terms *atonement*, *ransom*, and *redemption* in light of Christ's death and resurrection.

Form three groups to look at a selection of the week's readings. Group 1: Romans 5–6 (Day 3); Group 2: Philippians 2–3 (Day 4); and Group 3: 2 Corinthians 4–5 (Day 5). Ask each group to scan the assigned Scriptures for the purpose of discussing this question: According to Paul, how is Jesus' death and resurrection to take shape in the attitudes and actions of believers?

Examining God's Word in Context
(15 – 20 minutes)

A Gospel story about a life that begins by proclaiming "the kingdom of God is at hand" and ends by being nailed to a cross cannot be anything other than a life that matters, not just theologically but sociopolitically. The gospel, or good news, about Jesus has implications for the wider world.

Viewing the Video: Session 8, Part 2

Prepare to View Video:
Listen for what is said about how early Christians made sense of Jesus' death.

Discuss After Viewing Video:
How does our belief in Jesus' resurrection influence how we view his death? How does the way we make sense of Jesus' death affect how we live out our faith in community with others?

Going Forth with God's Word: An Invitation to Discipleship
(10 – 15 minutes)

Call attention to the paragraph on the cross-staff on page 91 of the participant book. The cross-staff was a navigational tool of the thirteenth through sixteenth centuries. A ship's pilot calculated his position and chartered his course by taking measurements of sun and stars with the cross-staff—lining up his reality with the cross. In pairs, discuss where you are in the sea of life. How does your reality line up with what Jesus' cross represents? How does your reality line up with what Jesus' resurrection represents?

Conclude the discussion by asking the pairs to share responses to this question: How does Jesus' dying and rising change the way you see yourself before God?

Closing and Prayer

Close with prayer.